Microsoft SharePoint

The Microsoft 365 Companion Series

Dr. Patrick Jones

OLYMPUS ACADEMY
PRESS

TABLE OF CONTENTS

Introduction to SharePoint: Unlocking Collaboration and
Organization...1

What Is SharePoint? 5

Why Use SharePoint?..9

Getting Started with SharePoint: Building Your Foundation 13

Best Practices for Using SharePoint Effectively 19

Tips and Tricks for Mastering SharePoint.............................25

Copilot in SharePoint: Unlocking AI-Powered Collaboration 31

Common Pitfalls When Using SharePoint and How to Avoid Them ..37

Sarah's SharePoint Transformation.....................................43

Summary and Reflection 47

Embracing the Power of SharePoint and Beyond......................51

INTRODUCTION TO SHAREPOINT: UNLOCKING COLLABORATION AND ORGANIZATION

Imagine stepping into a workspace where everything you need is at your fingertips—documents, project plans, communication tools—all organized, accessible, and secure. That's the promise of SharePoint. At its core, SharePoint is about connection: connecting people to the resources, information, and tools they need to succeed. Whether you're managing a team project, organizing company-wide content, or streamlining processes, SharePoint acts as a powerful digital hub.

For many, the idea of SharePoint might seem daunting at first. It's often associated with large enterprises or complex intranets, leaving smaller teams or individuals wondering if it's relevant to them. Spoiler alert: it absolutely is. SharePoint is as versatile as it is robust, adapting to the needs of organizations of all sizes. Whether you're part of a corporate team or a small business, SharePoint has something to offer.

This book is here to guide you through understanding and mastering SharePoint. Think of it as a friendly companion walking you through each step, breaking down the complexities into manageable, relatable lessons. Whether you're entirely new to SharePoint or you've dabbled but never fully embraced it, you're in the right place. Together, we'll explore how this tool can transform your workflows, enhance collaboration, and make your daily tasks more efficient.

In the chapters ahead, we'll delve deep into the world of SharePoint, starting with the basics. What exactly is SharePoint? How does it work? Why should you use it? These questions will lay the foundation for your journey, giving you the confidence to dive in and explore its many features.

We'll start with an overview of SharePoint's purpose and capabilities. From document libraries to team sites, you'll learn how SharePoint creates a centralized platform for sharing and storing information. The "Why Use SharePoint" chapter will illustrate its value with real-world examples, showcasing how it simplifies processes, enhances productivity, and fosters collaboration.

From there, we'll guide you through getting started with SharePoint, setting up sites, libraries, and lists that match your team's needs. You'll also discover best practices for keeping your content organized and secure, ensuring SharePoint becomes a helpful tool rather than a source of frustration.

If SharePoint feels like a labyrinth, think of this book as your map. Our goal is to make the concepts simple, approachable, and even fun to learn. Each chapter is designed with practical examples and clear explanations, so you can follow along step by step.

We'll also explore advanced features, like how AI-powered tools like Microsoft Copilot enhance your SharePoint experience, saving time and effort. You'll learn how to avoid common pitfalls that new users often encounter and how to use SharePoint's vast array of features without feeling overwhelmed.

But this book isn't just about the technical side of things. It's about transforming the way you work. SharePoint is more than a tool; it's a mindset—a way to streamline your workflows, collaborate effectively, and keep everything in its place. By the time you reach the final chapter, you'll see SharePoint not as a challenge to overcome but as a partner in your success.

In today's fast-paced, remote-first world, the ability to collaborate efficiently isn't just a luxury—it's a necessity. SharePoint was built with this reality in mind. It's designed to break down silos, making information accessible to everyone who needs it while maintaining strict control over permissions and security.

Consider a team scattered across different time zones, working on a product launch. SharePoint provides them with a shared space where they can access the latest files, communicate updates, and track progress—all in real-time. No more email chains, lost attachments, or version control nightmares. It's not just about convenience; it's about enabling teams to do their best work, no matter where they are.

And SharePoint isn't just for teams. It's for anyone looking to organize and streamline their workflows. Whether you're managing personal projects, coordinating a nonprofit, or running a small business, the principles we'll cover in this book apply to any context.

Throughout this book, you'll also follow the story of Sarah, a professional who, like many of us, started out feeling intimidated by SharePoint. Sarah's journey will mirror your own, offering relatable examples of how SharePoint can solve common challenges and improve everyday workflows. From learning the basics to mastering advanced features, Sarah's transformation will inspire you to embrace SharePoint's potential.

While this book focuses on SharePoint, it's important to remember that it's part of the broader Microsoft 365 ecosystem. Tools like Teams, OneDrive, and Planner integrate seamlessly with SharePoint, creating a connected environment that simplifies your work even further. As you explore SharePoint's features, you'll begin to see how it fits into the bigger picture and how its capabilities are enhanced by its connections to other tools.

If you've already explored other books in the Microsoft 365 Companion Series, you know that each tool has its strengths and specialties. SharePoint is no exception—it's a cornerstone of modern collaboration, and understanding how to use it effectively can elevate your work to new levels.

Learning SharePoint might feel like a big leap, but you're not alone. This book is here to guide you, step by step, through the process. By the time you're finished, you'll not only understand how SharePoint works but also how to make it work for you.

So, whether you're here to simplify your workflow, strengthen your team's collaboration, or just satisfy your curiosity, you're in the right place. Let's get started, and together, we'll unlock the full potential of SharePoint.

WHAT IS SHAREPOINT?

At its heart, SharePoint is a platform designed to simplify the way people store, share, and collaborate on information. Imagine a digital workspace where all your team's files, communication tools, and project data come together seamlessly. That's SharePoint—a hub for collaboration that's as versatile as it is powerful. But to truly understand SharePoint, we need to break it down into its key components and explore how it integrates with the broader Microsoft 365 ecosystem.

SharePoint is essentially a web-based platform that allows individuals and teams to create, organize, and manage content. Think of it as a digital headquarters where information flows freely but securely. Unlike a traditional file storage system, SharePoint combines document management with collaboration tools, workflow automation, and advanced search capabilities.

Here's a simplified way to think about SharePoint: it's like a Swiss Army knife for your organization's information needs. Whether you're managing files, running workflows, or hosting a company-wide intranet, SharePoint can adapt to fit your goals.

To understand SharePoint, it helps to break it down into its core functionalities:

1. **Document Libraries**
   Document libraries are the backbone of SharePoint. They store files in an organized, searchable structure. Unlike traditional folders, libraries come with built-in features like version history, metadata tagging, and permission controls, making it easy to manage content collaboratively.

2. **Lists**
   Lists in SharePoint are like spreadsheets on steroids. They allow you to store and track information in a structured way, with added features like workflows, custom views, and integration with apps like Power Automate and Power Apps.

3. **Sites**

   SharePoint sites are customizable spaces for teams or projects. You can create a site for a specific department, like Marketing, or for a company-wide initiative, like onboarding new employees. Each site can have its own document libraries, lists, calendars, and more.

4. **Intranets**

   For larger organizations, SharePoint often serves as an intranet—a centralized space where employees can access company news, policies, resources, and tools. It keeps everyone connected and informed, no matter where they are.

5. **Search**

   SharePoint's search capabilities are a game-changer. Instead of digging through countless folders, you can use keywords, metadata, or filters to find exactly what you need in seconds.

While SharePoint is a powerful tool on its own, its true potential shines when integrated with other Microsoft 365 apps. SharePoint isn't an isolated platform; it's deeply interconnected with tools like OneDrive, Teams, and Power Automate, forming a seamless ecosystem that supports modern work.

- **SharePoint and OneDrive**

  At first glance, SharePoint and OneDrive might seem similar—they both store files in the cloud. The key difference lies in their purpose. OneDrive is designed for personal file storage, while SharePoint is built for team collaboration. When you upload a file to a SharePoint site, it's accessible to everyone with permissions, making it ideal for shared projects. In contrast, OneDrive files are private unless you explicitly share them.

- **SharePoint and Teams**

  Microsoft Teams is a hub for communication and collaboration, and SharePoint is the engine powering its file-sharing capabilities. Every time you create a new team in Teams, a SharePoint site is automatically created in the background to store the team's files.

This tight integration ensures that documents shared in Teams channels are organized and accessible within SharePoint.

- **SharePoint and Power Automate**
  Power Automate, Microsoft's workflow automation tool, integrates seamlessly with SharePoint. You can set up automated processes, like sending an email when a file is updated or moving documents to specific folders based on their metadata.

- **SharePoint and Power Apps**
  With Power Apps, you can build custom applications that use SharePoint data as their foundation. For example, you could create an app to track employee onboarding tasks, with data stored in a SharePoint list.

To bring this to life, let's consider a few scenarios where SharePoint excels:

1. **A Marketing Team**
   The Marketing team at a company uses a SharePoint site to manage campaigns. The site includes document libraries for storing creative assets, a calendar for tracking deadlines, and a list for monitoring campaign progress. Team members upload new designs, update campaign statuses, and collaborate seamlessly—all within the SharePoint environment.

2. **An HR Department**
   The HR team uses SharePoint to host the company intranet. Employees can visit the intranet site to access resources like benefits documents, training materials, and company news. The HR team also uses a SharePoint list to track job applications and coordinate interviews.

3. **A Small Business**
   Even smaller organizations can benefit from SharePoint. A local consulting firm uses a SharePoint site to store client contracts, share project updates, and automate invoice approval workflows with Power Automate.

The beauty of SharePoint lies in its ability to adapt to different needs. Whether you're managing a simple team site or a complex organizational intranet, SharePoint provides the tools to make your processes more efficient. Its integration with other Microsoft 365 apps means you can connect your workflows and avoid the silos that often plague digital workspaces.

But SharePoint's value isn't just in its features—it's in how it empowers people. By centralizing information and making collaboration seamless, SharePoint allows teams to focus on what really matters: doing great work together.

Now that we've covered what SharePoint is and how it fits into the Microsoft 365 ecosystem, the next step is understanding why you should use it. In the next chapter, we'll dive into the specific benefits SharePoint offers, from streamlining collaboration to improving security. Whether you're managing files for a small team or building an intranet for an entire organization, you'll see how SharePoint can make a tangible difference in your work.

Let's continue the journey and uncover why SharePoint might just be the tool you've been looking for.

WHY USE SHAREPOINT?

If you've ever found yourself drowning in a sea of email attachments, struggling to track down the latest version of a file, or wondering how to bring your team's work together in one cohesive place, then you already understand the problems SharePoint is designed to solve. SharePoint isn't just another tool in the Microsoft 365 suite—it's a game-changer for collaboration, organization, and productivity.

In this chapter, we'll explore the key reasons why SharePoint stands out as a must-have solution for teams, organizations, and even individual users. Whether you're managing large projects, centralizing company resources, or simply trying to stay organized, SharePoint provides a wealth of features to simplify your work.

One of SharePoint's greatest strengths is its ability to centralize information. In many workplaces, documents and data are scattered across email threads, personal drives, and various cloud storage solutions. This fragmentation can lead to confusion, missed deadlines, and duplicated efforts.

With SharePoint, everything is stored in one place. Document libraries, lists, and shared sites ensure that team members always know where to find the latest version of a file or update. For example, instead of sifting through emails to locate a final report, you can simply access the SharePoint site where all project files are stored.

This concept of a "single source of truth" doesn't just improve efficiency—it builds trust. When everyone on the team knows they're working with accurate, up-to-date information, collaboration becomes smoother and more effective.

Collaboration is at the heart of SharePoint. The platform is designed to make teamwork effortless, no matter where your team members are located. Multiple people can work on the same document at the same time, with changes automatically saved and synced. This eliminates the chaos of version control and ensures that everyone is on the same page—literally.

Imagine you're part of a marketing team preparing a campaign proposal. With SharePoint, you and your colleagues can work together on the document in real-time, adding comments, making edits, and discussing ideas without stepping on each other's toes. The result? Faster turnaround times and better outcomes.

And collaboration doesn't stop with documents. SharePoint's integration with Microsoft Teams allows you to link team chat conversations directly to your SharePoint files. This means you can discuss a project in Teams while easily accessing all related files stored in SharePoint.

Every team and organization is unique, and SharePoint recognizes that. It offers unparalleled customization options to tailor the platform to your specific needs. Whether you're building a simple team site or a complex intranet, SharePoint gives you the tools to make it your own.

For example, you can design SharePoint sites that reflect your organization's branding, create custom workflows to automate repetitive tasks, and build dashboards that display real-time data. And as your team or organization grows, SharePoint scales with you. It's equally effective for small teams as it is for large enterprises with thousands of employees.

Another reason to use SharePoint is its seamless integration with the Microsoft 365 ecosystem. SharePoint doesn't exist in a silo—it's deeply connected to tools like OneDrive, Teams, Outlook, and Power Automate. This integration makes workflows more cohesive and reduces the friction that often comes with using multiple platforms.

For instance, when you create a new team in Microsoft Teams, a SharePoint site is automatically created in the background to store files shared within that team. Similarly, OneDrive syncs with SharePoint, allowing you to access team files from your personal drive without duplicating content.

This level of integration ensures that all your tools work together, creating a unified experience that enhances productivity and saves time.

In an era where data breaches and compliance requirements are top of mind, SharePoint stands out as a secure platform that prioritizes data protection. Built on Microsoft's robust cloud infrastructure, SharePoint includes advanced security features like encryption, multi-factor authentication, and detailed access controls.

SharePoint also helps organizations meet compliance standards by providing audit logs, retention policies, and data loss prevention tools. If you're handling sensitive information, these features give you peace of mind while ensuring that you remain compliant with industry regulations.

As an example, a healthcare organization using SharePoint can store patient records securely while controlling access based on roles and responsibilities. This ensures that only authorized personnel can view or edit sensitive data.

SharePoint's integration with Power Automate enables you to create workflows that simplify and automate routine tasks. Whether it's sending notifications when a document is updated, collecting approvals for a project proposal, or organizing incoming data, SharePoint workflows save time and reduce manual effort.

A procurement team using SharePoint to manage vendor contracts. Instead of manually tracking approvals, they set up a workflow in Power Automate that routes contracts to the appropriate stakeholders, sends reminders for pending approvals, and archives completed files—all automatically.

These workflows not only save time but also ensure consistency and accuracy in processes.

Have you ever spent half an hour searching for a single file, only to discover it was mislabeled or saved in the wrong folder? SharePoint eliminates this frustration with its powerful search capabilities. You can search by keywords, tags, or even metadata, and SharePoint will find exactly what you're looking for.

Better yet, SharePoint's search function extends across the entire platform. Whether the file is in a document library, a list, or even a

Teams channel linked to SharePoint, it's all accessible through one centralized search.

One of the reasons SharePoint is so versatile is its ability to serve different roles within an organization.

- For managers, SharePoint offers dashboards and reporting tools to track progress on projects.

- For team members, it provides a space to share ideas, collaborate on documents, and stay organized.

- For IT professionals, it's a secure, scalable platform that integrates with existing systems.

Whether you're leading a team or contributing to a project, SharePoint adapts to your role and enhances your productivity.

Sarah works as a project manager for a mid-sized tech company. Before SharePoint, her team relied on email chains and local file storage to collaborate, which often led to confusion and delays.

When Sarah introduced SharePoint, everything changed. She set up a SharePoint site for her team, complete with document libraries for project files, lists for tracking tasks, and a calendar for deadlines. The team quickly embraced the new system, and the results were immediate: fewer missed deadlines, more efficient collaboration, and a clearer picture of project progress.

Now, Sarah can't imagine managing projects without SharePoint. It's become her team's go-to platform for staying organized and productive.

SharePoint isn't just a tool—it's a way of working smarter. It helps you bring people, processes, and information together in one place, reducing inefficiencies and fostering collaboration. Whether you're managing a small team or leading a large organization, SharePoint provides the flexibility and power you need to succeed.

GETTING STARTED WITH SHAREPOINT: BUILDING YOUR FOUNDATION

Embarking on your SharePoint journey can feel like stepping into uncharted territory, but don't worry—you don't need to be an IT expert to get started. SharePoint's intuitive interface and customizable features make it accessible for teams and individuals alike. Whether you're setting up a team site, organizing files, or creating workflows, this chapter will guide you through the initial steps to build a solid foundation.

By the end of this chapter, you'll not only have your first SharePoint site up and running, but you'll also understand how to structure it for maximum efficiency and usability.

Before diving into the setup process, let's quickly revisit what SharePoint is. SharePoint is a web-based platform that acts as a central hub for storing, organizing, and sharing information. It's made up of sites, which are like virtual workspaces where you can manage files, collaborate with others, and create custom tools to streamline your workflow.

There are two main types of SharePoint sites:

1. **Team Sites:** Designed for collaboration among a specific group, like a department or project team. These sites focus on file sharing, communication, and teamwork.

2. **Communication Sites:** Created to share information broadly, such as a company-wide intranet or an event portal.

For most users, starting with a team site is the best approach.

Step 1: Creating Your First SharePoint Site

Getting your first SharePoint site up and running is straightforward. Here's how to do it:

1. **Access SharePoint:**
   Log in to your Microsoft 365 account and navigate to SharePoint from the app launcher (the grid of nine dots in the top-left corner).

2. **Choose "Create Site":**
   Once in SharePoint, you'll see the option to create a site. Select this to begin.

3. **Select Your Site Type:**
   Choose whether you want to create a Team Site or a Communication Site. For collaborative projects, start with a Team Site.

4. **Name Your Site:**
   Pick a name that reflects the purpose of your site, like "Marketing Team" or "Project Alpha." SharePoint will generate a site URL based on this name.

5. **Set Permissions:**
   Decide who can access your site. You can invite specific individuals or groups, and you'll also set whether they have editing or viewing rights.

6. **Add Your Site Description:**
   Provide a brief explanation of your site's purpose. This is especially helpful if you plan to share the site with a larger audience later.

7. **Click "Finish":**
   SharePoint will create your site, and you'll be taken to your new workspace.

Step 2: Structuring Your Site for Success

Once your site is created, it's time to customize it. The structure of your site will depend on your team's needs, but here are a few general tips:

- **Organize with Sections and Web Parts:**
  SharePoint sites are built using **web parts**, which are customizable building blocks. Add sections like document libraries, calendars, and task lists to organize your content.

- **Set Up Document Libraries:**
  A document library is where your team will store and manage files. You can create multiple libraries for different types of content, such as "Contracts," "Presentations," or "Training Materials."

- **Create Lists for Data Tracking:**
  If you need to track information like project statuses or contact lists, use SharePoint's list feature. Lists are like powerful spreadsheets with added functionality for filtering, sorting, and automating tasks.

- **Add a Home Page Welcome:**
  Make your home page inviting and functional by adding a welcome message, important links, or quick access to key resources.

Step 3: Adding and Managing Content

With your structure in place, it's time to start adding content.

- **Upload Files:**
  Drag and drop files directly into your document library or use the "Upload" button. SharePoint will handle version history automatically, so you never lose track of changes.

- **Organize with Folders and Metadata:**
  Use folders for a simple hierarchical structure or metadata for more advanced filtering and searching. For example, you can tag documents with keywords like "Urgent" or "2024 Campaign" to make them easier to find.

- **Set Permissions:**
  Control who can view or edit specific files or folders by adjusting permissions. For instance, you might allow your entire team to edit a draft report but restrict access to the final version.

Step 4: Introducing Your Team to SharePoint

One of the biggest challenges with any new tool is getting others to adopt it. SharePoint is no exception. Here's how to make the transition smoother:

- **Provide a Guided Tour:**
  Walk your team through the site, highlighting key features and showing them how to access and upload files.

- **Encourage Collaboration:**
  Show team members how to co-author documents in real-time and use comments for feedback.

- **Start Small:**
  Focus on one or two features initially, like document libraries or task lists, before introducing more complex tools like workflows or integrations.

Step 5: Connecting SharePoint to Other Tools

One of SharePoint's greatest strengths is its integration with the Microsoft 365 ecosystem.

- **Sync with OneDrive:**
  Use OneDrive to access SharePoint files on your desktop or mobile device. This allows you to work offline and sync changes automatically.

- **Link with Teams:**
  If your team uses Microsoft Teams, connect your SharePoint site

to a Teams channel. This makes it easy to access files and updates without switching apps.

- **Automate with Power Automate:**
  Create workflows to automate repetitive tasks, like sending notifications when a file is updated or approving document changes.

Step 6: Maintaining Your SharePoint Site

Setting up your site is just the beginning. To keep it running smoothly, follow these maintenance tips:

- **Review and Update Regularly:**
  Periodically review your site's content and structure to ensure it remains relevant and organized.

- **Monitor Usage:**
  Use SharePoint's built-in analytics to track how your site is being used and identify areas for improvement.

- **Seek Feedback:**
  Ask your team for input on what's working and what could be improved. SharePoint is most effective when it evolves alongside your team's needs.

Getting started with SharePoint is an exciting step, but it's just the beginning. In the next chapter, we'll explore best practices for managing your SharePoint site effectively, from maintaining organization to leveraging advanced features. By implementing these strategies, you'll ensure that your site becomes an indispensable tool for your team.

BEST PRACTICES FOR USING SHAREPOINT EFFECTIVELY

Mastering SharePoint isn't just about understanding its features—it's about using those features in ways that maximize efficiency, foster collaboration, and keep your content secure and organized. In this chapter, we'll cover essential best practices to help you and your team get the most out of SharePoint. Whether you're managing a simple team site or a company-wide intranet, these strategies will set you up for success.

1. Start with a Clear Purpose

Before diving into SharePoint, take a moment to define the purpose of your site. Is it for a specific project, department, or company-wide initiative? Having a clear goal ensures that your site's structure, content, and features align with its intended use.

- **Example:** If your site is for a product launch, focus on features like a document library for marketing materials, a task list for deadlines, and a calendar for events.

When your team understands the site's purpose, they're more likely to use it effectively.

2. Keep It Simple

SharePoint is incredibly flexible, which can sometimes lead to overcomplicated setups. Resist the urge to create too many folders, libraries, or lists. Simplicity is key to ensuring your site remains user-friendly.

- **Use Metadata Instead of Nested Folders:** Metadata allows you to tag files with attributes like "Client Name" or "Project Stage," making it easier to filter and search for content without digging through endless folders.

- **Limit Libraries and Lists:** Only create new libraries or lists when they serve a distinct purpose.

Pro Tip: Periodically review your site to identify and eliminate clutter, ensuring it remains easy to navigate.

3. Organize Content Thoughtfully

The way you organize your site has a huge impact on its usability. Use a logical structure that mirrors how your team works.

- **Group Content by Function or Topic:** Create sections or libraries for categories like "Team Documents," "Policies," or "Marketing Assets."
- **Use Descriptive Names:** Avoid generic names like "Folder 1" or "Misc." Instead, use clear labels like "2024 Product Launch" or "HR Training Materials."

Example: A sales team might have libraries for "Client Proposals," "Contracts," and "Sales Reports," making it easy for team members to find what they need.

4. Encourage Collaboration

SharePoint's strength lies in its ability to bring teams together. Encourage collaboration by leveraging features like real-time co-authoring, comments, and notifications.

- **Set Up Shared Libraries:** Ensure all team members have access to the right libraries. Assign permissions to avoid accidental edits or deletions.
- **Use Alerts and Notifications:** Enable alerts to inform team members when files are updated or tasks are assigned.

Pro Tip: Integrate your SharePoint site with Microsoft Teams to enhance collaboration further, linking documents directly to your Teams channels.

5. Establish Permissions Carefully

One of SharePoint's greatest advantages is its granular permission settings, but improper use can lead to security risks or confusion.

- **Role-Based Permissions:** Assign permissions based on roles. For instance, project managers might have editing rights, while other team members only have viewing rights.

- **Use Groups for Permissions:** Instead of assigning permissions to individuals, create groups like "Marketing Team" or "HR Managers" to streamline management.

Example: On a SharePoint site for client work, you might allow the design team to edit files while restricting access to the legal team for review purposes only.

6. Leverage Templates and Standardization

Consistency is crucial for making SharePoint sites intuitive and user-friendly. SharePoint offers templates for sites, lists, and pages, which you can customize to suit your team's needs.

- **Create Custom Templates:** If your team frequently creates similar types of content, design a custom template for documents, workflows, or lists.

- **Standardize Naming Conventions:** Agree on a consistent format for file and folder names, like "YYYY-MM-DD_ProjectName_DocumentType."

Pro Tip: Document these standards in a "How to Use This Site" page on your SharePoint site to ensure everyone is on the same page.

7. Regularly Review and Update Content

A SharePoint site is only as useful as the content it contains. Outdated or irrelevant information can lead to confusion and clutter.

- **Schedule Routine Cleanups:** Set a calendar reminder to review your site quarterly or semi-annually. Archive or delete old files, update lists, and reorganize as needed.

- **Use Version History:** SharePoint automatically tracks changes to files, so you can always revert to a previous version if needed.

Example: An HR team might archive job descriptions for filled positions and update onboarding materials to reflect the latest company policies.

8. Integrate with the Microsoft 365 Ecosystem

SharePoint shines when used alongside other Microsoft 365 apps. Take advantage of integrations to streamline workflows and improve collaboration.

- **Sync Files with OneDrive:** Enable OneDrive syncing for offline access to SharePoint libraries.

- **Automate Tasks with Power Automate:** Create workflows to automate processes like sending notifications, approving requests, or moving files based on metadata.

- **Enhance Collaboration with Teams:** Link SharePoint libraries to Teams channels for easy access to files during discussions.

Pro Tip: Explore Power Apps to build custom applications that leverage SharePoint data, like tracking project statuses or managing inventory.

9. Train Your Team

Even the most well-designed SharePoint site won't succeed if your team doesn't know how to use it. Invest time in training to ensure everyone understands the platform's features and benefits.

- **Host Guided Tours:** Walk team members through the site, highlighting key features and explaining how to perform common tasks.

- **Provide Documentation:** Create a quick-reference guide or a FAQ page on your SharePoint site.

- **Encourage Experimentation:** Let team members explore features like tags, alerts, and workflows on their own to build confidence.

10. Monitor Site Performance and Feedback

To keep improving your SharePoint site, monitor its usage and gather feedback from your team.

- **Use Analytics:** SharePoint includes built-in analytics that show how users interact with the site, helping you identify what's working and what needs improvement.

- **Listen to Your Team:** Encourage team members to share suggestions or report issues, and act on their feedback to enhance the site's functionality.

Example: If analytics show that certain libraries are rarely accessed, consider reorganizing or consolidating them to improve usability.

By following these best practices, you'll create a SharePoint site that's not only functional but also intuitive and engaging. Remember, SharePoint is a dynamic tool—it thrives when regularly maintained and adapted to meet your team's evolving needs.

TIPS AND TRICKS FOR MASTERING SHAREPOINT

SharePoint is a robust platform with a wealth of features, but even seasoned users often overlook some of its most useful capabilities. In this chapter, we'll explore tips and tricks that can help you work smarter, not harder. These insights will help you uncover hidden features, speed up tasks, and make the most of your SharePoint experience.

Whether you're managing files, collaborating with a team, or designing a SharePoint site, these tips will give you a practical edge and deepen your mastery of this powerful tool.

1. Use Metadata for Smarter Organization

Folders are familiar and intuitive, but they're not always the most efficient way to organize files in SharePoint. Metadata—data about your data—offers a better solution by letting you tag files with attributes like "Project," "Client," or "Priority."

- **How It Works:** Instead of burying a file in a folder, you can tag it with relevant metadata. This allows you to filter and search for files based on those tags, no matter where they're located.

- **Example:** Sarah, a project manager, tags her documents with "Project Phase" and "Team Member Responsible." When she needs to find all files related to the planning phase of a project, she filters by that tag instead of hunting through folders.

Pro Tip: Create custom metadata columns for document libraries to reflect your team's unique needs.

2. Leverage Version History

One of SharePoint's most underrated features is its ability to track version history for every document. This means you can always revert to an earlier version if changes are made by mistake.

- **How It Works:** Right-click on a document and select "Version History." You'll see a list of past versions, complete with timestamps and the names of the people who made changes.

- **Example:** During a campaign launch, Sarah's team accidentally overwrites a critical file. Using version history, she restores the previous version in seconds.

Pro Tip: Encourage your team to rely on version history instead of saving multiple copies of a file with names like "FINAL_FINAL.docx."

3. Master Advanced Search

The search bar in SharePoint is more powerful than it looks. By using advanced search techniques, you can locate files, lists, or data with precision.

- **How It Works:** Use specific keywords, filters, or Boolean operators (like AND, OR, NOT) to narrow your search results.

- **Example:** Sarah searches for a file created by her colleague John in the past month. She types Author:John AND Modified:ThisMonth into the search bar and finds the file instantly.

Pro Tip: Save frequent searches as bookmarks for quick access.

4. Customize Your View

SharePoint allows you to create custom views for lists and libraries, tailoring how information is displayed to meet your needs.

- **How It Works:** Use filters, sorting, and grouping options to create views that highlight the most relevant data. For example, you can create a view that shows only overdue tasks or files modified in the last week.

- **Example:** Sarah sets up a custom view in her task list to display only items assigned to her, sorted by due date.

Pro Tip: Share custom views with your team to improve collaboration and consistency.

5. Automate Tasks with Power Automate

SharePoint's integration with Power Automate opens the door to countless automation possibilities. Automating repetitive tasks can save you time and reduce errors.

- **How It Works:** Create workflows that trigger actions based on events in SharePoint, like sending an email when a file is updated or moving files to a specific folder.

- **Example:** Sarah automates her document approval process. When a file is uploaded to a specific library, Power Automate sends an approval request to her manager and moves the file to the "Approved" folder once it's signed off.

Pro Tip: Start with Power Automate's templates to quickly set up common workflows.

6. Sync Libraries with OneDrive

For quick and easy access to SharePoint files, sync your document libraries with OneDrive. This lets you open, edit, and save files directly from your desktop or mobile device.

- **How It Works:** Click the "Sync" button in any document library to create a local folder on your device that mirrors the library's contents. Changes sync automatically.

- **Example:** Sarah works offline during a flight, editing files in her synced OneDrive folder. Once she reconnects to the internet, her changes are automatically updated in SharePoint.

Pro Tip: Use OneDrive's selective sync feature to choose which folders you want to sync, saving storage space on your device.

7. Use Alerts to Stay Informed

Stay on top of updates by setting up alerts for changes to files, lists, or libraries.

- **How It Works:** Right-click on a file or list and select "Alert Me." You'll receive notifications when changes are made.

- **Example:** Sarah sets up an alert for her team's document library. Anytime a file is updated, she gets an email notification, ensuring she's always in the loop.

Pro Tip: Customize alerts to receive notifications immediately, daily, or weekly, depending on your preferences.

8. Explore Web Parts for Dynamic Pages

Web parts are customizable building blocks that add functionality to your SharePoint pages. Use them to display content dynamically, like news updates, charts, or quick links.

- **How It Works:** On any page, click "Edit" and add web parts from the toolbox.

- **Example:** Sarah adds a news web part to her SharePoint homepage to display the latest team announcements and updates.

Pro Tip: Experiment with the "Highlighted Content" web part to automatically display documents or pages that meet specific criteria.

9. Simplify Collaboration with Teams Integration

If your team uses Microsoft Teams, you can link SharePoint libraries directly to Teams channels.

- **How It Works:** In Teams, navigate to the Files tab of any channel and link it to your SharePoint library. This ensures that everyone has access to shared files without switching apps.

- **Example:** Sarah links her SharePoint project site to her team's "Campaigns" channel in Teams, making collaboration seamless.

Pro Tip: Use Teams' chat feature to discuss SharePoint files in real time, fostering quicker decision-making.

10. Make Use of Templates

Templates can save you time and provide consistency when creating new SharePoint sites, pages, or lists.

- **How It Works:** SharePoint offers pre-designed templates for common use cases, like project management or employee onboarding.

- **Example:** Sarah uses the "Project Site" template to quickly set up a new site for an upcoming product launch, complete with task lists, calendars, and document libraries.

Pro Tip: Customize templates to fit your organization's specific needs, then reuse them for future projects.

By incorporating these tips and tricks into your workflow, you'll unlock new levels of productivity and efficiency in SharePoint. These small changes can have a big impact, helping you save time, reduce frustration, and get the most out of the platform.

COPILOT IN SHAREPOINT: UNLOCKING AI-POWERED COLLABORATION

In today's fast-paced digital workplace, the sheer volume of information we handle can be overwhelming. SharePoint has long been a trusted tool for organizing, sharing, and collaborating, but now it's taking things to the next level with the introduction of Microsoft Copilot. By harnessing the power of artificial intelligence, Copilot in SharePoint helps you work smarter, faster, and with greater confidence.

This chapter will explore how Copilot enhances SharePoint's capabilities, turning your sites and libraries into intelligent, dynamic workspaces. Whether you're a seasoned SharePoint user or just getting started, Copilot is here to make your experience even more productive and seamless.

At its core, Microsoft Copilot is an AI-powered assistant designed to enhance your productivity across the Microsoft 365 ecosystem. When integrated with SharePoint, Copilot goes beyond traditional search and organization features to offer intelligent suggestions, streamline tasks, and help you find insights buried within your content.

Imagine asking Copilot to summarize a document library, create a new site based on your preferences, or analyze project data stored in lists. It's like having a personal assistant who knows the ins and outs of your SharePoint environment, ready to lend a hand at a moment's notice.

Copilot transforms the way you interact with SharePoint by making complex tasks easier and time-consuming processes faster. Let's explore its key features:

1. Intelligent Search and Summarization

Searching for content in SharePoint is now more intuitive and efficient with Copilot's AI-driven capabilities. Beyond finding files or documents, Copilot can summarize the content of entire libraries or lists, helping you quickly identify the information you need.

- **Example:** Sarah, a marketing manager, needs an overview of all campaign documents in her SharePoint site. Instead of scanning each file, she asks Copilot, "Summarize the key takeaways from the Marketing Campaigns library." Within seconds, she has a concise summary of the latest documents.

Pro Tip: Use prompts like "Show me the files updated last week" or "Find all documents tagged with 'Urgent.'"

2. Automated Site Creation

Building a new SharePoint site from scratch can be time-intensive, especially if you're unsure where to start. Copilot simplifies this process by guiding you through site creation based on your specific needs.

- **Example:** Sarah's team needs a new site for an upcoming product launch. She tells Copilot, "Create a site for the product launch with sections for timelines, files, and task tracking." Copilot generates a fully functional site with the required structure in minutes.

Pro Tip: Experiment with prompts like "Set up a team site for collaboration" or "Create a communication site for sharing company news."

3. Content Organization and Cleanup

Over time, SharePoint sites can become cluttered with outdated files, redundant documents, or poorly organized content. Copilot helps you streamline your libraries and lists by identifying duplicates, suggesting folder structures, and archiving old files.

- **Example:** Sarah's team's SharePoint site is overflowing with unused files. She asks Copilot, "Find and suggest which files haven't been accessed in six months," and quickly archives the irrelevant ones.

Pro Tip: Schedule regular content reviews with Copilot to maintain an organized workspace.

4. Workflow Automation

Copilot integrates seamlessly with Power Automate to simplify repetitive tasks. From sending notifications to managing approvals, Copilot can help set up and optimize workflows tailored to your needs.

- **Example:** Sarah wants to ensure her team stays on top of document approvals. She asks Copilot, "Set up a workflow to notify managers when a new file is added to the 'Approval Needed' folder," and the process is automated instantly.

Pro Tip: Combine Copilot and Power Automate to create workflows for common tasks like updating task lists or archiving completed projects.

5. Data Insights and Analysis

If your SharePoint site includes lists or data-heavy libraries, Copilot can analyze the information and provide actionable insights. From identifying trends to generating reports, it's a powerful tool for making data-driven decisions.

- **Example:** Sarah tracks campaign performance using a SharePoint list. She asks Copilot, "What are the most common campaign challenges noted this quarter?" Copilot analyzes the data and highlights recurring issues.

Pro Tip: Use Copilot to create visualizations or summaries for team presentations, saving time and effort.

6. Enhanced Collaboration

Collaboration is at the heart of SharePoint, and Copilot makes it even better by facilitating real-time updates, suggesting file-sharing options, and summarizing team activities.

- **Example:** Sarah's team is preparing for a presentation. She asks Copilot, "What updates were made to the campaign presentation this week?" and gets a detailed summary of changes made by her colleagues.

Pro Tip: Use Copilot to track collaboration history and highlight key contributions during team reviews.

Using Copilot in SharePoint is simple, but getting the most out of it requires a little practice. Here's how to get started:

1. **Enable Copilot:** Ensure your organization has access to Microsoft Copilot and that it's enabled for SharePoint. Speak to your IT administrator if you're unsure.

2. **Start with Prompts:** Use natural language to interact with Copilot. Ask questions or describe tasks you need help with, such as "Summarize this document library" or "Create a workflow for task approvals."

3. **Refine Your Approach:** Copilot learns from your input, so the more you use it, the better it gets at understanding your needs.

4. **Explore Integrations:** Combine Copilot with other Microsoft 365 tools like Teams, OneDrive, and Power Automate for an even more cohesive experience.

To make the most of Copilot's capabilities, keep these tips in mind:

- **Be Specific:** The more detailed your prompts, the more accurate Copilot's responses will be.

- **Experiment Freely:** Don't hesitate to try new commands or explore features you haven't used before.

- **Involve Your Team:** Encourage your team to use Copilot collaboratively, sharing insights and tips to maximize its potential.

Copilot in SharePoint isn't just a feature—it's a paradigm shift in how we work. By combining the power of AI with the flexibility of SharePoint, Copilot enables you to focus on what truly matters: creating, collaborating, and achieving your goals.

COMMON PITFALLS WHEN USING SHAREPOINT AND HOW TO AVOID THEM

SharePoint is a powerful tool, but like any technology, it can present challenges if not used thoughtfully. Many users, especially those new to the platform, encounter common pitfalls that can hinder productivity, create frustration, or lead to messy and unmanageable sites. The good news? With a bit of foresight and strategy, these issues are entirely avoidable.

In this chapter, we'll explore some of the most common mistakes people make with SharePoint and provide practical tips to help you steer clear of them. By learning from these potential missteps, you can ensure a smoother, more efficient experience for yourself and your team.

1. Overcomplicating Site Structure

One of the most frequent issues with SharePoint is an overly complex site structure. It's tempting to create layers upon layers of folders, subfolders, and libraries to organize your content, but this often leads to confusion and difficulty in finding files.

- **The Pitfall:** Excessive folders or an inconsistent organizational scheme can make your site difficult to navigate. Users may waste time hunting for files or create duplicates if they can't find what they need.

- **How to Avoid It:**
    - Opt for metadata tagging instead of deep folder structures. Metadata allows you to categorize files with attributes like "Project Name" or "File Type," making them easier to filter and search.

- Stick to a logical, consistent structure that mirrors your team's workflows. For example, group files by project or department rather than by individual contributors.

- Periodically review your site structure to ensure it remains streamlined and relevant.

2. Neglecting Permissions Management

SharePoint's granular permission settings are a blessing, but they can quickly become a curse if mismanaged. Improper permissions can lead to accidental data exposure or prevent team members from accessing the files they need.

- **The Pitfall:** Assigning permissions to individuals instead of groups can result in a tangled web of access controls that are difficult to manage.

- **How to Avoid It:**

  - Use role-based groups (e.g., "Marketing Team" or "Managers") to assign permissions instead of individual users.

  - Regularly audit permissions to ensure they're still appropriate. Remove access for users who no longer need it, such as employees who have left the team.

  - Apply the principle of least privilege—only grant the level of access necessary for a user's role.

3. Failing to Maintain and Update Content

A SharePoint site is only as useful as the content it contains. Over time, outdated files, irrelevant documents, and unused lists can clutter your site, making it harder to find current and accurate information.

- **The Pitfall:** Allowing your site to become a "digital junk drawer" reduces its effectiveness and frustrates users.

- **How to Avoid It:**

    o Schedule regular content reviews to identify outdated files and archive or delete them as needed.

    o Use version history to track changes and ensure that only the most current documents are visible.

    o Implement metadata to mark files with expiration dates or review deadlines.

4. Ignoring Training and Onboarding

SharePoint's robust feature set can be overwhelming for new users, leading to underutilization or misuse of the platform.

- **The Pitfall:** Without proper training, team members may stick to old habits (like emailing files back and forth) or fail to take advantage of SharePoint's capabilities.

- **How to Avoid It:**

    o Offer hands-on training sessions and walkthroughs for new users. Highlight key features like version history, tagging, and sharing.

    o Create a "How to Use This Site" page with FAQs, tutorials, and best practices tailored to your team's needs.

    o Encourage users to explore and experiment with SharePoint's features to build confidence.

5. Overloading Libraries and Lists

It's easy to let document libraries and lists grow unchecked, especially when multiple team members are contributing content.

- **The Pitfall:** Overloaded libraries and lists can slow down site performance and make it harder to locate files or data.

- **How to Avoid It:**

  o Set up multiple libraries or lists for different purposes rather than cramming everything into one.

  o Use filters and views to display only the most relevant content for a specific audience or task.

  o Establish clear guidelines for file naming and metadata usage to keep things organized.

6. Overlooking Integration Opportunities

SharePoint is most effective when used in conjunction with other Microsoft 365 tools, but many users fail to leverage these integrations.

- **The Pitfall:** Treating SharePoint as a standalone tool limits its potential and forces users to juggle multiple platforms unnecessarily.

- **How to Avoid It:**

  o Sync SharePoint libraries with OneDrive for offline access to files.

  o Integrate SharePoint with Teams to create a seamless collaboration experience.

  o Automate repetitive tasks with Power Automate, such as sending reminders or archiving completed projects.

7. Mismanaging Search Settings

SharePoint's search feature is powerful, but it requires proper setup to deliver accurate and relevant results.

- **The Pitfall:** Without configured metadata and search filters, users may struggle to find what they're looking for, leading to frustration and inefficiency.

- **How to Avoid It:**

    o Use metadata consistently across your site to improve search accuracy.

    o Customize search results pages to highlight the most relevant files or lists.

    o Educate users on advanced search techniques, like using Boolean operators or filters.

8. Failing to Monitor Site Usage

Without monitoring how your SharePoint site is being used, you risk missing opportunities to improve or identify potential problems.

- **The Pitfall:** A lack of analytics makes it difficult to understand which features are working and which aren't.

- **How to Avoid It:**

    o Use SharePoint's built-in analytics tools to track user activity, file access, and site performance.

    o Identify underutilized areas of your site and assess whether they can be improved or removed.

    o Gather feedback from your team to understand their needs and challenges.

9. Overcomplicating Automation

While automation can save time, overly complex workflows can backfire, leading to errors or confusion.

- **The Pitfall:** Automations that are too intricate can become difficult to troubleshoot or maintain.

- **How to Avoid It:**

    o Start with simple workflows and expand them as needed.

    o Test workflows thoroughly before rolling them out to your team.

    o Document each workflow's purpose and setup for future reference.

10. Neglecting to Adapt Over Time

SharePoint isn't a "set it and forget it" platform. As your team's needs evolve, your SharePoint site must adapt to stay relevant.

- **The Pitfall:** A static site becomes less useful as processes change or new challenges emerge.

- **How to Avoid It:**

    o Regularly evaluate your site's structure, content, and features to ensure they align with current goals.

    o Stay informed about new SharePoint updates and features that could benefit your team.

    o Encourage an open feedback loop with your team to identify areas for improvement.

By understanding and avoiding these common pitfalls, you'll ensure that your SharePoint site remains a valuable asset for your team. The key is to approach SharePoint with a mindset of continuous improvement—reviewing, refining, and evolving your setup as your needs change.

SARAH'S SHAREPOINT TRANSFORMATION

Sarah leaned back in her chair, staring at her computer screen. Her project management job had always been busy, but lately, it felt unmanageable. Email chains were out of control, files were scattered across various platforms, and her team was struggling to collaborate effectively. Deadlines were looming, and Sarah knew she needed a solution. That's when her IT department introduced her to SharePoint.

At first, Sarah was skeptical. She had heard of SharePoint but assumed it was a tool for IT professionals or large corporations. She couldn't see how it would help her small, fast-paced team. But with a bit of guidance, Sarah decided to give it a shot—and what followed was a transformation that changed how she worked forever.

Before SharePoint, Sarah's workflow was a patchwork of inefficiencies. Her team relied on email to share files, often leading to version control nightmares. Someone would edit a document, save it with a new name, and email it back to the group. Within a week, there were five versions of the same file, each with slight differences, and no one knew which was the final one.

Meetings were another headache. Sarah spent hours digging through email threads to find attachments, manually updating task lists, and juggling separate calendars for each project. Collaboration felt like a chore rather than a seamless process.

She knew there had to be a better way.

With help from her IT team, Sarah set up her first SharePoint site. They started small, focusing on a single project to keep things manageable. The site included a document library for files, a task list to track progress, and a shared calendar for deadlines.

As Sarah explored SharePoint, she began to see its potential. She could tag documents with metadata, making them searchable by category, date, or project phase. Instead of hunting for files, she could type a few keywords into the search bar and find exactly what she needed.

The IT team also showed her how to set up permissions. She created a group for her core team with editing rights and another for stakeholders who needed view-only access. No more accidental edits or misplaced files—it was a game-changer.

One afternoon, Sarah faced a critical deadline. Her team was preparing a presentation for a client, and tensions were high. Previously, managing such a project would have been a nightmare of scattered files and last-minute email chains. But this time, everything was different.

Using SharePoint, Sarah uploaded the draft presentation to the document library and shared the link with her team. Everyone could access the same file and make edits in real-time. Changes were tracked automatically, so Sarah didn't have to worry about losing important updates.

She also used the task list to assign roles: John would refine the slides, Maria would proofread, and Sarah would compile feedback. The shared calendar kept everyone aligned on deadlines, and alerts notified the team when updates were made.

For the first time, Sarah felt in control. The project came together smoothly, and the client presentation was a success.

As Sarah grew more comfortable with SharePoint, she began exploring its integrations with Power Automate. One of her biggest frustrations had been manually tracking document approvals, a task that often slipped through the cracks.

With Power Automate, Sarah created a workflow that notified her manager whenever a file was uploaded to the "Approvals" folder. Once approved, the workflow automatically moved the document to the "Final" folder and sent a confirmation email to Sarah. What used to take hours now happened in minutes.

She also set up automated reminders for overdue tasks in the task list. Her team no longer had to remember every detail—SharePoint handled it for them.

When Microsoft Copilot was introduced to SharePoint, Sarah was hesitant at first. Could AI really improve an already efficient system? But after trying it, she was blown away.

One day, Sarah needed to summarize a document library filled with reports from various projects. Instead of scanning each file, she asked Copilot, "Summarize the key insights from this library." Within seconds, she had a concise overview that she could share with her team.

Copilot also helped her create new sites. When Sarah's team started a new project, she simply told Copilot, "Set up a site for the '2024 Campaign' with sections for documents, timelines, and team tasks." The site was ready in minutes, tailored to her specifications.

For Sarah, Copilot became a trusted partner, handling repetitive tasks and providing insights that saved her time and energy.

Six months after adopting SharePoint, Sarah's workflow looked entirely different. Her team no longer relied on messy email threads or scattered file systems. Instead, they worked collaboratively in a centralized, organized space. Meetings were more productive, projects ran more smoothly, and Sarah had reclaimed hours of her time.

What surprised Sarah most was how adaptable SharePoint was. Whether managing a small project or coordinating a company-wide initiative, the platform scaled to meet her needs. And with tools like Copilot and Power Automate, she felt equipped to handle any challenge that came her way.

Sarah's journey with SharePoint mirrors the experience many users have when they first dive into the platform. It can feel overwhelming at first, but with persistence and a willingness to learn, SharePoint becomes more than just a tool—it becomes a cornerstone of productivity and collaboration.

As you explore SharePoint, remember that every feature is designed to make your work easier and more efficient. Start small, experiment with different tools, and don't be afraid to ask for help. Like Sarah, you'll soon discover that SharePoint isn't just a solution to today's challenges—it's a foundation for future success.

SUMMARY AND REFLECTION

As we wrap up this journey through SharePoint, it's time to reflect on what we've learned and how it all ties together. SharePoint is much more than a platform for storing and sharing files—it's a dynamic, adaptable tool that empowers individuals and teams to work more efficiently, collaborate seamlessly, and stay organized in an increasingly complex digital world.

In this book, we've explored the many facets of SharePoint, breaking it down into actionable insights and practical guidance:

- **Introduction to SharePoint:** We started by understanding what SharePoint is—a digital hub that connects people, files, and workflows in one cohesive space.

- **Why Use SharePoint:** We highlighted its ability to centralize information, enhance collaboration, and integrate with other Microsoft 365 tools.

- **Getting Started:** From creating your first site to structuring it effectively, you learned the foundational steps to build a SharePoint workspace that works for you.

- **Best Practices:** We shared strategies for keeping your site organized, secure, and user-friendly, ensuring it remains a valuable asset over time.

- **Tips and Tricks:** Advanced features like metadata tagging, custom views, and Power Automate integrations revealed how SharePoint can simplify your work even further.

- **Copilot in SharePoint:** We explored how AI-powered Copilot enhances the platform, offering intelligent suggestions, automating tasks, and unlocking insights you didn't know you had.

- **Common Pitfalls:** By understanding the challenges users often face, you gained tools to avoid them and maintain a productive SharePoint environment.

Each chapter built on the last, creating a comprehensive guide to mastering SharePoint. But this book isn't just about the technical details—it's about transformation.

Sarah's experience with SharePoint is a reflection of what many users encounter. She started from a place of frustration, where scattered files and inefficient processes made her work more challenging than it needed to be. Through determination and a willingness to learn, she transformed her workflow and unlocked the full potential of SharePoint.

Sarah's journey illustrates key lessons that resonate with all of us:

- **Start Small:** Just as Sarah began with one project site, you don't need to tackle every SharePoint feature at once. Focus on the basics, and let your skills grow naturally over time.

- **Embrace Collaboration:** By bringing her team into the process, Sarah showed how SharePoint fosters a culture of shared responsibility and transparency.

- **Leverage Technology:** Tools like Power Automate and Copilot enabled Sarah to automate repetitive tasks and focus on what truly mattered, reminding us that technology is here to enhance—not replace—our capabilities.

- **Stay Adaptable:** As her needs evolved, Sarah continually refined her SharePoint setup, demonstrating that flexibility is key to long-term success.

Just like Sarah, you have the opportunity to make SharePoint your own. Whether you're managing team projects, organizing personal workflows, or coordinating across departments, the principles and tools outlined in this book can help you navigate your challenges and achieve your goals.

Reflect on where you are in your SharePoint journey:

- Are you just starting out, learning to create your first site?

- Have you already built a site but want to take it to the next level with advanced features?

- Or are you looking for ways to streamline existing workflows and bring more people into the fold?

Wherever you are, remember that SharePoint isn't just a tool—it's a resource for growth, a way to bring order to chaos, and a platform for collaboration and innovation.

While this book focuses on SharePoint, it's important to recognize its place within the broader Microsoft 365 ecosystem. SharePoint doesn't operate in isolation; it connects seamlessly with tools like Teams, OneDrive, Power Automate, and Copilot, creating a unified environment that supports modern work.

Consider how you can integrate SharePoint with these tools to amplify its impact:

- Use Teams for real-time collaboration while relying on SharePoint to organize and store shared files.

- Sync SharePoint libraries with OneDrive for offline access and easier file management.

- Automate workflows with Power Automate to save time and reduce manual effort.

- Leverage Copilot to gain insights, streamline site creation, and simplify complex tasks.

Each of these integrations builds on SharePoint's strengths, helping you create a connected, efficient digital workspace.

Sarah's journey and your own path with SharePoint remind us of the power of learning and adaptation. It's not just about mastering a tool—it's about embracing a mindset that prioritizes growth, collaboration, and efficiency. The lessons you've learned here don't end with SharePoint.

They can be applied to any challenge you face, whether it's adopting new technology, leading a team, or improving your personal workflows.

As you move forward, keep the following in mind:

- Stay curious. There's always more to learn, especially as tools like SharePoint continue to evolve.

- Be patient. Mastery takes time, and every step forward is progress.

- Share your knowledge. By helping others embrace SharePoint, you reinforce your own skills and contribute to a culture of collaboration.

This book is part of the Microsoft 365 Companion Series, a collection designed to help you unlock the potential of tools like SharePoint, OneDrive, Teams, and more. If you've found this guide helpful, consider exploring other books in the series to continue your learning journey.

Your experience with SharePoint is just the beginning. The skills, insights, and strategies you've gained here are stepping stones to even greater accomplishments. Whether you're building your next SharePoint site, integrating it with Teams, or exploring new features in Microsoft 365, you have the tools to succeed.

Thank you for letting this book be a part of your journey. Now, go forth and make SharePoint—and your work—truly extraordinary.

EMBRACING THE POWER OF SHAREPOINT AND BEYOND

As we close this book, it's worth reflecting on the transformative potential of SharePoint—not just as a tool, but as a catalyst for better collaboration, organization, and productivity. SharePoint has proven itself to be a cornerstone of the modern digital workplace, bridging gaps between people, processes, and technology.

But this journey doesn't end here. The insights and skills you've gained from mastering SharePoint are only the beginning. As part of the Microsoft 365 ecosystem, SharePoint connects seamlessly with other tools, creating endless possibilities for innovation and growth.

If there's one key takeaway from this book, it's that SharePoint is as much about people as it is about technology. It brings teams together, fosters transparency, and simplifies complex workflows. By centralizing information and making it accessible, SharePoint helps you and your team focus on what truly matters: creating, collaborating, and achieving your goals.

You've learned to:

- Set up and structure SharePoint sites tailored to your needs.
- Use best practices to keep your site organized and efficient.
- Leverage advanced features, like metadata and automation, to save time.
- Tap into the power of Microsoft Copilot to enhance productivity with AI-driven insights.

Whether you're just starting your SharePoint journey or refining your existing workflows, you now have the tools and confidence to make the platform work for you.

As robust as SharePoint is, its true strength lies in its integration with other Microsoft 365 apps. SharePoint doesn't exist in isolation—it's part of a larger ecosystem designed to support every aspect of your work.

Consider how these tools complement SharePoint:

- **Teams:** Seamlessly link files and collaborate in real-time.

- **OneDrive:** Sync SharePoint libraries for offline access and personal file management.

- **Power Automate:** Automate repetitive tasks and streamline workflows.

- **Copilot:** Unlock AI-powered insights across your SharePoint sites and beyond.

By combining these tools, you can create a connected, cohesive workspace that adapts to your needs and grows with your goals.

The world of technology is constantly evolving, and SharePoint is no exception. Microsoft frequently introduces updates and new features, offering opportunities to enhance your workflows and discover new possibilities. Staying curious and open to learning is key to making the most of what SharePoint—and the broader Microsoft 365 ecosystem—has to offer.

- **Explore new features:** Keep an eye out for SharePoint updates, like enhanced integrations or AI-powered tools.

- **Experiment with integrations:** Try connecting SharePoint to other apps you use, such as Planner or Power Apps, to see how they can work together.

- **Share your knowledge:** Teach your team or organization what you've learned, fostering a culture of collaboration and innovation.

This book is part of the Microsoft 365 Companion Series, which aims to provide practical, approachable guides to the tools that empower modern work. If SharePoint has sparked your interest in exploring other Microsoft 365 apps, you're in the right place.

Consider diving into:

- **OneDrive:** Master personal file storage and collaboration.
- **Teams:** Unlock the power of communication and real-time teamwork.
- **Copilot:** Discover AI-driven productivity across Microsoft 365.
- **Planner:** Organize and track tasks for personal and team projects.

Each tool offers unique capabilities, and understanding how they work together can elevate your productivity to new heights.

Sarah's journey through SharePoint mirrors the experience of many users: initial hesitation, gradual learning, and eventual transformation. Like Sarah, you've taken the time to understand SharePoint's features, adapt them to your needs, and embrace its potential to simplify your work and empower your team.

Think about how far you've come, not just in mastering a platform, but in adopting a mindset of growth, collaboration, and continuous improvement. That mindset will serve you well as you tackle new challenges, adopt new tools, and explore new opportunities.

Thank you for joining this journey through SharePoint. Writing this book has been a privilege, and I hope it has provided you with valuable insights, practical tools, and the inspiration to take your work to the next level.

Remember: SharePoint is more than just a tool—it's a foundation for innovation, collaboration, and success. Whether you're building your next site, exploring new features, or diving into other Microsoft 365 tools, the skills you've gained here will serve as a springboard for what's next.

www.ingramcontent.com/pod-product-compliance
Lightning Source LLC
LaVergne TN
LVHW052323060326
832902LV00023B/4559